BAK FRITAY
HAITIAN STREET FOODS

NATACHA GOMEZ

First printing, 2021

United States of America

ISBN: 9798717197618

BAK FRITAY

Table of Contents

DEDICATION vii

GRANNY CIENNE.. vii

ACKNOWLEDGEMENTS viii

INTRODUCTION x

ABOUT STREET FOODS xi

DEEP FRYING BASICS xii

BASIC KNIFE "CUTS" xiii

EXTRA TIPS.. xv

    HAITIAN HOT PICKLED SLAW (PIKLIZ) 3

    CREAMY COCONUT SAUCE (VINÈG LÈT) 5

    MOLASSES & RHUM RAISIN SAUCE (SIWO WÒM REZEN) 7

    BOUILLON CUBES (KIB EPIS LAKAY) 9

    HAITIAN BLENDED SPICES (EPIS HAITI) 11

    ACCRAS WITH TAINO DIP (ACCRAS TAINO) 15

    COW PEAS ACCRAS (ACCRAS PWA NEG) 17

    FRIED HERRING PATTIES (PATE KODE ARAN) 19

    FRIED PLANTAINS (BANNANN FRI) 21

    CHICKEN FRITTERS (MARINAD POUL) 23

    FRIED CHICKEN (POUL FRI) 25

    FRIED KACHKI FISH (PISKET FRI) 27

    LABADEE BEACH'S FRIED FISH (PWASON FRI LABADEE) 29

    FRIED FRESHWATER FISH (KABO FRI) 31

    FRIED OCTOPUS (CHATWOUJ FRI) 33

    GELEE'S FRIED LOBSTER (OMA FRI LANME GELEE) 35

    CAP-HAÏTIEN FRIED PORK (GRIOT OKAP) 37

    SCRAMBLED EGGS WITH OYSTERS FROM AQUIN 41

    BOILED BREADFRUIT (LAM BOUYI) 43

    HAITIAN NATIONAL RICE (DIRI PWA KOLE) 45

    SPICY COW COD SOUP (JANJOL OR BEGA) 47

    SAUTÉED WHELKS (BRIGOT OU BOURGOT) 49

    GRILLED CONCH (LAMBI GRIYE) 51

KACHKI IN CREOLE SAUCE (PISKET NAN SÒS) 53

SAUTÉED CURED GOAT (SESIN KABRIT) 55

HAÏTIAN BEEF POTAGE (BOUYON BÈF) 57

STEAMED CORNMEAL PUDDING (ABLIN/ AKASAN FEY) 61

RUSTIC COCONUT COOKIES (KOKONET) 63

GRANNY CIENNE BUTTER COOKIES 65

COCONUT FUDGE (DOUS KOKOYE) 67

HAÏTIAN DUKUNU (DUKUNU) 69

MILK CHEESE & CURDLED MILK (FROMAJ LÈT AK LÈT KAYE) 71

MILK FUDGE (DOUS LÈT) 73

PEANUT FUDGE (DOUS PISTACH) 75

CANDIED COCONUT (TABLET KOKOYE) 77

CANDIED SESAME SEEDS (TABLET ROROLI) 79

CANDIED ROASTED CASHEWS (TABLET NWA GRYE) 81

CANDIED PEANUTS (TABLET PISTACH ARCAHAIE) 83

PEANUTS NOUGAT (NOUGA PISTACH) 85

TAINO CRAB DIP (SÒS CRAB TAINO) 87

DEDICATION

There are no words I could say that would thank you enough for the patience

and the support you have given me throughout my career.

This is yet another hat added to my collection.

With you by my side, I know I will reach the moon!

Thank you again, Keisha and Giovanni.

GRANNY CIENNE

My grandmother Lucienne, on the paternal side, played a big role in my love for cooking. As a toddler, I was already helping her bake her cookies. At 8, I already had my vegetable garden and my special corner in her big kitchen. The table and stovetop we're adjusted for my height.

I remember her teaching me and helping me know about the products first. How to feel the fruits or vegetables, how to touch, to smell them... Just before the taste. For her, it was all about quality and freshness. Those products coming from our land tasted better because I knew where they were from; the labor, the love, and effort that was put into growing and caring for them. And from these lands we owned, each season would come the land workers with fresh produce. Coconuts, fruits, vegetables, meats, and different spices and herbs. I would enjoy learning from these men and women, knowing about their life and their productions. This was a real treat for me.

Granny Cienne would also bring me to visit these lands. She would tell tales of the family's past generations, little anecdotes. All these great memorable times spent with her fueled my love for the products of our lands and our city.

Today, I bring you a piece of her and a piece of my present family as we go over the recipes and recall information from aunties and uncles as well as mom and dad! This, and future books, are a family affair!

Please enjoy!

Natacha

ACKNOWLEDGEMENTS

I love to share what I know, my research, my memories.

This series of our beloved street food started as a thank you to all that paved the way in promoting our gastronomy.

First, I want to thank Jehovah for the gift of life and creativity.

To Franck, thank you for encouraging me to always move forward.

To Keisha, my awesome daughter, PR, video producer, and co-host thank you for the countless hours by my side.

To Giovanni, my son, who is always there for me. A good taster too!

To my brother, who always believes in me and my goals, biggest supporter ever.

To my Mom and Dad, the co-editors. Thank you for all the advice, thank you for showing us that hard work always pays off.

To my friend Jonathan, for my logo, artwork, and website.

To Vickie my superwoman friend, without you I could not make it, thank you is not enough it is a pleasure to have you with me on this adventure.

To JK Photography, the pictures are amazing thank you again.

Enjoy this 100% manjé lokal book! (IG: 100_lokal)

PICKLED ONIONS HOT SAUCE

INTRODUCTION

I started my culinary journey by exploring the roots of tradition and modernity and how they intertwine. Later, when I did my first food festival to promote local and new Haitian gastronomy, our group chose the logo of the "Pilon" and a "Chef toque". It was a tangible way for people to understand what we were promoting.

Remembering my trips to Port-au-Prince in the '90s, I always included a quick stop at the street vendors' stalls of Delmas 31. They were situated in front of Chef Tony's Restaurant. I also made a point to visit other reputable places such as Kay Nerva in Delmas 33, the stalls in Kenscoff, Fermathe, and 5 Coins. Though street food hails from humble beginnings, it is enjoyed by the masses. It contributes to a traditional gastronomic experience for tourists and locals alike.

I had the privilege to talk to Gilbert Andre about the 5 coins experience. It is a story of a single restaurant that became an empire.

N.G.: Gilbert tell us about the beginning of 5 Coins?

G.A.: "The restaurant specializes in Haitian Fried Food "Fritay". Founded in July '92 by my father Joacin Andre. The first location was on Avenue Magloire Ambroise. It was named "5 Coins" because the restaurant was exactly situated at an intersection of 5 streets, thus "5 corners". Today we are famous for our "Pikliz Zonyon", and our "Accras". We are recognized as a reference brand. We presently have 6 locations in the capital; however, the project continues."

N.G: What is your favorite combo?

G.A.: "I like the *griot, bannann dous peze* ak *Pikliz zonyon*."

N.G.: What is the contribution of the New generation to 5 coins?

G.A.: "The new generation has bridged their innovations with the elders' experiences. The latest technology, social media networks, now play a major role in modernizing and revolutionizing the face of the brand. Our customer service personnel is trained on how they receive and treat orders. We strive to ensure the brand's sustainability, adapt to the current life, and keep true to our originality."

N.G: Nowadays, dishes are perpetually reimagined and refined. Street food provides the rawness and authenticity that we crave. It gives us such comfort because it strikes a chord within us that reminds us of home. With this cookbook, I invite you into my own home and offer you a gateway to a key part of the Haitian culture. Hoping that you truly find as much joy in these recipes that I have had in writing them. Please, remember to keep cooking with love.

ABOUT STREET FOODS

We have included recipes of regular "bak fritay" foods, as well as a few staples of street foods; this should give you an idea of our rich gastronomy. This part 1 of the New Haïtian Gastronomy cookbook series is simply an introduction to the dishes to come.

From the paradise that we call the "Ayiti pre-Columbus", we love the outdoors. "BBQ" was invented by the Taino and is derived from the word Barbacoa. We, islanders, enjoy the outdoors. We sit outside on our front porch, or front steps if in the city; we walk to get to places, we just walk up to the neighbor's doorsteps and start a conversation. Everything happens out in the open. We only use cars for long-distance rides or if we are carrying something heavy. We enjoy a walk in the parks to talk with friends or to see people passing by. A lazy Sunday is spent at the beach or in our backyard with friends and family.

In Haïti, we also know that our "griot" (*gree-oh*) has another taste when it is bought from street vendors. Anything really, bought from a street vendor has an exotic taste to it. Some street food vendors have the "arosé"; a type of rice served with the meat sauce of the day. It is a serving of cheap food but oh so full of flavor!

Back in the days, our hard-working African ancestors developed ways to adapt the crops at hand with the flavors of Africa. With little time to eat between hard labors, Sunday afternoons were the gathering of the slaves to cook and enjoy some free time. They used a "3 woch dife" *(burning wood between 3 rocks)* to cook on outside their "cases" (quarters); staples such as "patat ak lèt", "patat boukannen", "tchenchen" "zòrèy kochon boukannen", *(sweet potatoes and milk, fire-roasted sweet potatoes, cornmeal with spinach, fire-roasted pig ears)* while telling stories and chanting.

Eating from street vendors is part of our cultural heritage.

DEEP FRYING BASICS

Oil:

Use the right type of oil when frying your food. All oils do not give the same flavor. The best oil is peanut oil. If you cannot find it, choose an oil with a high smoking point like shortening frying oil or Rice Bran oil.

It is time to change your oil when it starts to smell, smoke at normal cooking temperature, foam, or burns the food even if the temperature is at the right level

Temperatures:

This is key to deep frying. If your oil is not at the right temperature, your food will come out soggy, overcooked on the outside, and uncooked on the inside.

Always follow the recommended setting for your deep fryer. If you use a deep heavy pan, temperatures should be between the 350F-400F range. Invest in a cooking thermometer.

Deep fryer, or Frying Pot size:

Use the right size of a deep fryer or heavy frying pot for your food.

Fill your fryer or heavy pot with the right amount of oil. Always leave about 3 inches between the oil and the top of the fryer or pot. (even more if what you are frying is heavy).

And please, please, yes, I said it twice... need I emphasize it more? Please keep water out of the hot oil to avoid splatter and getting yourself burnt. It is not just your arm; your eyes could be injured as well.

KEEP YOUR FINGERS AWAY from the oil, you are not made of steel. Use a fryer basket or a slotted spoon, or tongs to add, turn, or remove food from the oil.

Start early enough to avoid rushing, thus avoiding an overload of food into your fryer or pot. Cook small batches. It will cook faster and evenly.

Let the oil cool down completely before moving the fryer or pot to empty it and clean it. Please, do not discard the used oil into the sink or toilet. It will clog the pipes. Ask your city Town Hall or visit www.greencitizen.com for how-to-dispose-of-cooking-oil.

BASIC KNIFE "CUTS"

In this book I use the basic terms used in cooking: "diced", "chopped", "minced", "julienne" or "french cut", "brunoise", "enfilade", etc. Here is how to make them.

Large diced/chopped	an item cut into ¾-inch squares. This cut is used for everything from onions to watermelon to meat
Medium diced	an item cut into ½-inch squares. (e.g., "diced tomatoes", when no mention of size, a medium dice is good)
Small diced	an item cut into ¼-inch squares. (e.g., 1 cup celery diced small) Soup bases with celery, carrots, onions, etc., will use that cut.
Brunoise	an item cut into ⅛-inch squares. This cut is used when you want to garnish a dish.
Julienne	An item cut in long strips of ⅛-inch thickness. Carrots, cucumbers, potatoes, tomatoes, or other veggies are cut this way to put on top of another dish or be in a salad.
Chiffonade	The leaves are stacked rolled and cut thinly to form the thin strips. Leaves like basil, spinach, etc...
Minced	Smaller than a brunoise. It is a fine dice. Usually, garlic is minced. But you can also mince onions and shallots. This cut ensures that more flavor is released in a short period of cooking or marinating.

HOW TO USE AND PROPERLY CARE FOR A KNIFE: Use a cutting board/ use the proper knife for the right kind of job. Holding and using your knife properly will help you work more efficiently in a kitchen, respecting the size and cut helps in 'even' cooking and presentation. When cutting foods, always place them in a stable position. Guide the knife blade against the food with your free hand. Protect your fingertips by curling them inwards, using your knuckles to guide your knife.

You can store your knives in 3 basic ways depending on how your kitchen is set. Wall-mounted, drawer inserts or countertop knife blocks. These are safe ways if used correctly. I advise you to sharpen your knives regularly, wash them after use, and never leave them in a full sink; this could result in someone getting cut. Please let a knife fall without catching it, and lastly, wash knives by hand and dry with a cloth.

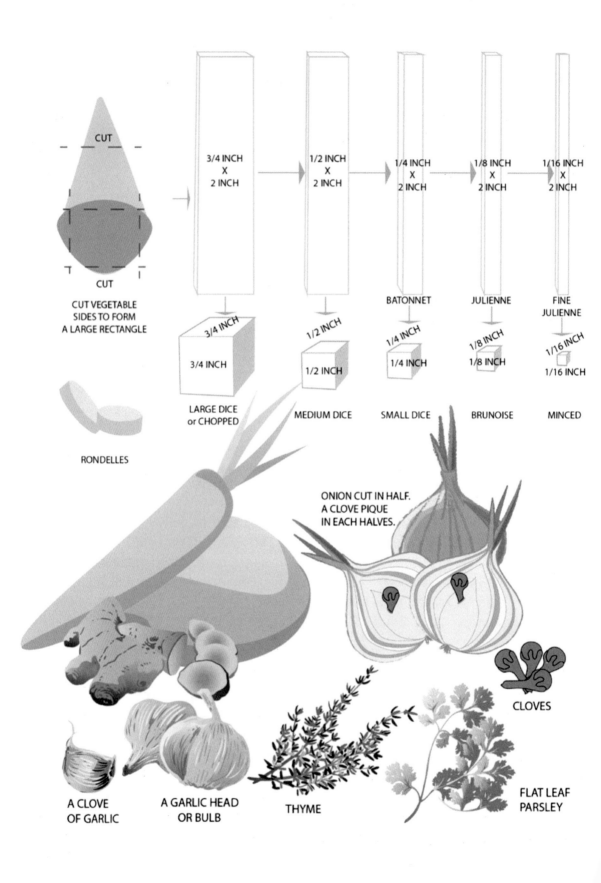

CUT

CUT

CUT VEGETABLE
SIDES TO FORM
A LARGE RECTANGLE

RONDELLES

3/4 INCH
X
2 INCH

1/2 INCH
X
2 INCH

1/4 INCH
X
2 INCH

1/8 INCH
X
2 INCH

1/16 INCH
X
2 INCH

BATONNET

JULIENNE

FINE
JULIENNE

3/4 INCH

3/4 INCH

1/2 INCH

1/2 INCH

1/4 INCH

1/4 INCH

1/8 INCH

1/8 INCH

1/16 INCH

1/16 INCH

LARGE DICE
or CHOPPED

MEDIUM DICE

SMALL DICE

BRUNOISE

MINCED

ONION CUT IN HALF.
A CLOVE PIQUE
IN EACH HALVES.

CLOVES

A CLOVE
OF GARLIC

A GARLIC HEAD
OR BULB

THYME

FLAT LEAF
PARSLEY

EXTRA TIPS

First... take a glass of wine or hot cocoa and relax while reading this:

AFRICAN BIRD CHILE: A variety of capsicum were exported from the new world to the old world by the Spanish and the Portuguese. The Portuguese brought these small and searingly hot chiles to Africa where they came to be known as pili-pili or Piri-Piri, Piman zwazo in Haïti, and were rapidly embraced. It is also a generic term for extremely hot powdered dried red chile used in Far Eastern cuisine.

ANNATTO OIL: An infused oil colored and slightly flavored by the seeds of the Achiote tree. Known in Haïti as roucou. The Taino women used it as a lip tint, as well as for their skin. To make the oil, heat 1 cup of oil or lard over medium heat and add 2 ounces of annatto seeds. Make sure not to fry the seeds to keep from getting a burnt taste. Cook for 2 to 5 minutes or until the oil turns a deep orange. Let it cool before you strain and discard the seeds. Store in a clean glass container.

It is used primarily to color foods cooked with oil in the Caribbean and Latin America. You make Annatto water to color your dishes as you would with saffron or turmeric; simmer the seeds in water for 2 to 5 minutes covered, allow the seeds to cool, strain, and discard them. Cracking the seeds before simmering produces a more intense color.

BEAT: Stirring rapidly in a circular motion, using a whisk, spoon, or mixer.

BITTER ORANGE OR SOUR ORANGE: Also known as the Seville orange. It is used in the Caribbean, Latin America, The Mediterranean, and parts of England to make marmalade. The juice is fruity and sour. If sour orange is not available, substitute with 3 parts of orange juice or grapefruit juice, 2 parts lemon or lime juice, and 1 part grapefruit zest.

BOUQUET GARNI: A french term referring to a bundle of herbs either tied together with string or twine or wrapped in cheesecloth to aid in removal after infusing stocks or sauces. The herbs and spices can be fresh or dried. Usually, parsley and parsley sprigs, thyme, and bay leaves are part of a bouquet garni.

CARAMELIZE: To slowly cook food until it turns sweet, nutty, and brown. You can also "caramelize" sugar, or cook it until it melts, becoming golden-brown, sweet, and thick. You can caramelize chopped onion by gently cooking it in butter or oil, usually for a long time at a low temperature. The sugars in the onion will begin to brown and become sweet.

CASSAVA: A long tuberous starchy root. An essential ingredient in many Latin American and Caribbean cuisines. Eaten mashed, added to stews, and used to make flatbread and chips. Cassava, also known as yuca (manioc) must be cooked or pressed before it is eaten, as it is poisonous in its raw form. Cassava flatbread is made from finely grated hard-pressed cassava meat.

Eaten fresh from the cassava makers with peanut butter, smoked herring chicktay, salé aranso, sesin kabrit, or griot. After a day or two, toast it in the oven and you get yourself a fresh, crisp piece of bread to lather your favorite bites. Cassava flatbread comes in different flavors such as sweet coconut, smoked herring, peanut, and garlic.

COW COD, HOW TO CLEAN IT:
If you bought fresh uncleaned cow cod from the meat market, remove the fat, the long vein on its side, and the skin and discard them. Remove the testicles around the cow cod. Cut open the Cod on the long side and clean it with lime and sour orange juices. Rinse with fresh water and drain. Now, medium dice the Cod meat, marinate overnight in lime and sour orange juice. The testicles should be cooked at the very last minute as they are very tender and tend to dissolve if cooked too long.

CRAB, HOW TO OPEN IT:
Cook the crab in a court bouillon (water, white wine, vegetables, and seasonings to taste) beforehand. Turn the crab on its back, pull the abdomen and tail to extract them and separate them from the trunk. Break the tongs with the nutcracker.

Extract the flesh from the pincers, the legs, and the chest with a seafood fork.

CHICKEN (WHOLE), HOW TO CUT IT:
(a sharp *chef's knife* makes cutting easier, and a separate cutting board for meat helps avoid cross-contamination. These steps also work for a cooked chicken). With chicken breast side up, pull each leg away from the body, then slice through skin between breast and drumstick.

Turn chicken on its side. Bend each leg back until the Thighbone pops out of its socket. Cut through the joint and skin to detach the leg completely. With chicken on its backside, pull each wing away from the body. Cut through the joint and remove the wing. Separate the breast from the back and save the back to make chicken stock.

Lift chicken and cut down through the rib cage and then shoulder joints to place breast skin side down. Split center bone using a chopping motion, then slice through meat and skin to separate into 2 pieces. To cut breast halves into quarters, turn each skin side up and cut in half diagonally through bone. To divide the legs, turn each skin side down and cut through joints (along the white fat line) You should end up with 6 to 10 parts, depending on whether you divided the breast halves and legs.

COCONUT MILK:
Extracted from the flesh of the coconut fruit. At home, get a ripe coconut from the market, open the hole, and extract the coconut water. Then crack open the hard shell, remove the meat. Grate it finely. Blend it with the coconut water and strain it… tasty coconut milk in minutes! You can always add more water to the strained meat and blend again to get the last bit of milk out.

CONCH, HOW TO CLEAN IT:
Starting with conch in their shells, break them gently so as not to cut the meat inside. Rinse under running water with either papaya leaves or parchment paper to remove the glue (a slimy substance). (the papain in papaya leaves breaks down connective tissues of meat, thus rendering it tender). Now, cut off the "foot" and all the black/grey or pinkish tough skin. Left with the firm white meat, you need to remove the "antenna", cut it open and discard the red membrane. Inside the main white meat, there is a white membrane, discard it.

Quickly rinse once more under cold running water. Use sour orange juice (not lime or lemon). Pat dry with a paper towel. Cut the meat into pieces, place them in a bowl, and use a meat tenderizer (too much will render the meat flaky). Cook in a pressure cooker for 25 minutes with leeks, onions, and ¼ cup of oil and water to cover the meat (NO SALT).

If you use a regular pot, use 8 to 10 cups of water per 2 pounds of meat. Cook on low-medium heat for 1 to 2 hours.

CHOP, CUBE, DICE: Please see "Basic Knife Cuts".

DUKUNU: An ancient recipe brought to us through songs and tales from the Garifuna people. No written recipes from back in these times. The Garifuna lived along the Caribbean coasts of northern America. Move forward in time, and you get different versions of this easy-to-carry sweet cornmeal. This is mostly due to the unsteady access to ingredients within the slave population. Adding raisins came after their freedom. Dukunu is a distant cousin of the tamales. Today, cornmeal flour is mixed with green plantains, bananas, yuccas, or sweet potatoes.

DUST: To coat lightly with powdery ingredients, such as Confectioners' sugar or cocoa.

FRYING: Cooking your food in oil or another fat. Pan-fried foods are generally turned over once or twice during cooking, using tongs or a spatula. Sautéed foods are cooked by "tossing in the pan".

JULIENNE: please see "Basic Knife Cuts".

KNEAD THE DOUGH: Mixing the dough with the hands or a mixer.

MARINATE: The process of soaking meat, poultry, or fish in a sauce or flavored liquid for a specified period.

PAPAYA PIKLIZ: A condiment in Haitian cuisine of green papaya cut in fine julienne, salt, carrots, scotch bonnet peppers. It is often seasoned with cut shallots, 1 whole clove, and pickled in white vinegar. It is very spicy.

PIMAN KONFI/ PICKLED PEPPERS: Use a mix of scotch bonnet peppers and African bird peppers, cut shallots, roughly chopped carrots, 3 whole cloves, salt, 2 whole black pepper with enough white vinegar and sour orange juice to completely cover all the ingredients in a glass container. Leave about an inch of space on top of the liquid as the peppers will ferment. Cover tightly for 15 days in a cool place. Use for soups or to marinate meat.

PLANTAIN: A type of banana that is starchy longer and thicker. It is sweet only when overripe and it is always cooked before eaten. Plantain is considered gluten-free.

PLANTAIN LEAVES: Are used as a vessel in the Caribbean to marinate or cook meat or fish, e.g.: tamales, ablin, and dukunu. It is also used to cover half-cooked rice for the last 25 minutes of cooking.

PREPPING OCTOPUS: You can always purchase cleaned ones at the fish market. Or, as a self-doer, you can tackle this easily. Start by slicing off the heads of the fresh octopuses and discarding them. Remove all the internal organs, turn the flesh inside out to remove the innards, and cut any membranes. Discard them. Flip it back, remove the eyes; spread the tentacles to remove the beak by cutting, in a circular motion, around it and push it out with your thumb. Tenderize the octopuses with a meat mallet. Rinse under cold running water and reserve. You want to do this the day before you cook them. Refrigerate.

SAUTÉ/ SAUTÉED: A dry heat method of cooking food that uses a small amount of oil or fat in a shallow pan over relatively high heat.

SHUCKING OYSTER: Look at the oyster. It has a cupped side and a flatter side. Hold the oyster with a kitchen towel or oven mitt with the flatter side up. The cupped side holds the oyster and its liquid while you shuck/open it. Look for the hinge—where the shells are joined. Insert the knife there but be careful not to jam it too far or you might puncture the stomach and ruin the flavor. Now "pop" it open by twisting the knife blade.

SIMMER: Bring liquids to a boil, then reduce the heat until there are no bubbles forming.

SLICE: Please see "Basic Knife Cuts".

SCOTCH BONNET PEPPER: Slightly smaller than the habanero. Identical in heat rating of 100,000–350,000 Scoville units. However, the Scotch bonnet is sweeter, which is important in the overall flavor of the Caribbean meals.

SEA SALT: Salt that has been evaporated from seawater usually in the form of crystal or flakes. "Fleur de sel" (the finest of salt or salt blossom) are the distinctive pyramid-shaped crystals that rise to the top during the evaporation process and gathered first. "Sea salt" is what is left after evaporating all the seawater.

SESIN (SALTED/CURED GOAT): Since salting/ curing your meat is a long process, you should do more than one serving and have it for other occasions. Now, Slice 5lbs of goat meat as thinly as possible and add it to a bowl with 1 cup of coarse salt, juice of 2 sour oranges, and a sliced scotch bonnet pepper. Leave it in the fridge overnight. The next day, remove the meat from the liquid and pat dry with a paper towel. Heat your oven to 200ºF [93 ºC]. Place the meat on a cookie rack and dry in the oven until the meat is quite stiff and dry to the touch (it takes about 3 to 4 hours). Let the meat cool to room temperature and store it in a sealed bag in the refrigerator for up to a month.

WHISK: To beat ingredients with a fork or a whisk.

ZEST: Finely grated or scrapped peels of unwaxed lemon, lime, orange, and citron.

SAUCES & SPICES

HAÏTIAN HOT PICKLED SLAW

ABOUT THIS RECIPE

Please, with or without gloves, do not touch your eyes or face while you are handling the hot peppers. Do not forget to wash the utensils and cutting board after use.

Servings: 04

10-15 minutes

Condiment

HAITIAN HOT PICKLED SLAW (PIKLIZ)

INGREDIENTS

- 1 cup julienne-cut green beans
- 1 cup bitter orange juice
- ¼ cup lime juice
- 2 tbsp sea salt
- 2 cups shredded cabbage
- 1 cup shredded carrots
- 3 Tbsp of water
- 15 scotch bonnet peppers
- 5 bird peppers (green or red)

PREP & COOK

1. Clean and cut all the peppers thinly and use the seeds.
2. Cut all the vegetables in Julienne, then measure recipe quantities.
3. In a bowl, mix the peppers with the vegetables, then add the juices of sour orange, lime, and water.
4. You can enjoy it now or wait an hour to let the juices infuse with the peppers.

TIPS

For a pop of color, use the green, yellow, orange, and red scotch bonnet peppers.

"Pikliz" adds texture and flavors to sandwiches. It is also great with rice, especially our Haïtian national rice.

Always use a clean spoon to keep your "Pikliz" fresh for days.

Please do not confuse "Pikliz" with "Piman Konfi" or "Vinèg Lèt".

A Caribbean and food lover must have. This traditional hot sauce was disappearing from our food repertoire.

CREAMY COCONUT SAUCE (VINÈG LÈT)

INGREDIENTS

1 cup Coconut Milk

1 small onion diced

1 clove of garlic

6 scotch bonnet peppers

1 tbsp coconut oil

5 tbsp of sour orange juice

Salt to taste

PREP & COOK

1. In a saucepan, fry, on medium heat, the diced onion in the coconut oil until translucent.

2. Then, blend the onions with coconut milk, salt, garlic, and scotch bonnet peppers.

3. Add the sour orange juice last, and blend for 30 seconds more.

TIPS

"Vinèg Lèt" is commonly eaten with boiled breadfruit (*Lame Bouyi*) sold by street food vendors in Haïti. They also sell grilled or boiled corn on the cob, cornmeal and spinach, breadfruit nuts with avocado.

You can also serve this sauce with any boiled or grilled seafood.

Try it on grilled conch... the sweet taste of it will be enhanced.

My mom says it is also a great addition to Brigot.

MOLASSES & RHUM RAISIN SAUCE

ABOUT THIS RECIPE
RUM vs RHUM: most rums (Demerara rum) are distilled from fermented molasses; rhum (rhum Agricole) is made from fresh-pressed sugar cane juice. Our own Rhum Barbancourt is a rhum Agricole.

Servings: 04

2 minutes + 30 minutes wait

Condiment

MOLASSES & RHUM RAISIN SAUCE (SIWO WÒM REZEN)

INGREDIENTS

- 1 tsp finely cut fresh ginger
- 1 tsp butter (not margarine)
- ½ cup molasses
- ¼ cup dark rum
- 3 tbsp dried raisins

PREP & COOK

1. In a saucepan, add the dark rum to the dried raisins. Reserve this mix for at least 20 minutes.

2. Now combine the molasses, ginger, and rum raisins. Cook on high heat for 1 minute. Keep stirring to avoid burning the sauce.

3. Remove from heat and whisk in the butter until well incorporated.

TIPS

Raisins in rum… 20 minutes is enough marinating time if you are in a hurry.
But, one hour will let the raisins absorb and double in size.
I like it that way and I add more rum/rhum, that is just me.
You can also use that sauce over vanilla ice cream… just let it cool as not to melt the ice cream.
I am just imagining it onto a cheesecake… I would just let the sauce thicken a bit.
Please, feel free to use the rhum Agricole, Barbancourt, if you can find it.
After all, this is a recipe from a Haitian Chef…

BOUILLON CUBES

ABOUT THIS RECIPE
The best way to ensure what goes into flavoring your food is to make it yourself. You can even withhold the salt if you like.
I do not promote the use of spices containing MSG.

Servings: 04

7 hours

Blended Spice

BOUILLON CUBES (KIB EPIS LAKAY)

INGREDIENTS

VEGETABLE BROTH

- 3 lbs. of chicken bones
- 1 big onion halved. Insert 1 clove (jiwof) in each half
- 1 head of garlic with peel
- 2 carrots peeled and cut in 2
- 2 celery stalks cut in 2
- 12 thyme sprigs
- 1 bunch of parsley with stem
- 2 bay leaves

BOUILLON CUBES

- 1 cup of the stock
- 1 tbsp curcumin (turmeric)
- 2 medium leeks (white part)
- 1 medium carrot
- 1 celery stalk
- 1 small onion
- ½ cup flat-leaf parsley
- 2 tbsp sea salt
- 2 garlic cloves
- 1 chive
- 1 big shallot

PREP & COOK

1. In a pot, place all the ingredients from the stock list. Then, add water to cover the ingredients at least 3 inches.
2. Cook on high heat until bubbles form, then lower the heat to low and let simmer uncovered for 4-6 hours. Every 15 min. skim the scum of the stock.
3. Once cooked, remove from heat, strain ingredients out of the stock. Cool the stock, and then refrigerate. THE NEXT DAY... remove the white grease floating on top of the stock.
4. Remove 1 cup for the cubes. Store the rest in clean glass containers.
5. Blend the ingredients for the cubes adding the cup of stock. Process until smooth.
6. Pour into an ice cube tray and freeze. When frozen, remove the cubes and put them into a Ziplock bag for storage.

TIPS

This broth can be made anytime you have leftover chicken or beef bones. You can use it for soups, sauces, rice. It adds great flavor to your dishes.

HAITIAN BLENDED SPICE

ABOUT THIS RECIPE

This is a basic blend of the spices we use in our daily cooking. Each cuisine cook can adjust to the household tastebuds.
I like garlic, so I add more.
I do not promote the use of spices containing MSG.

Servings: 6-12

20 minutes

Spice blend

HAITIAN BLENDED SPICES (EPIS HAITI)

INGREDIENTS

- 1 bunch of parsley
- 1 head of garlic, peeled
- 2 big shallots or 12 Haitian ones
- ½ tsp of cloves
- 1 green bell pepper, no seeds
- ½ tsp of black pepper
- ½ scotch bonnet pepper
- 2 chives
- Salt to taste

PREP & COOK

1. Peel the garlic. (remove the green germ if you do not like the taste. A darker and longer green germ stem has a more pungent taste).
2. Clean and roughly cut all spices into 2 or 3 parts.
3. Mix all ingredients in a food processor until you reach a fine paste.
4. Keep refrigerated.

TIPS

<u>What you could add:</u>
Sour orange juice- meat/poultry marinade. (place in the refrigerator for up to 24hours)
Lime juice- fish and shellfish marinade.
Vinegar- help it stay fresh for up to 10 days in the refrigerator.
You can also store it in an ice cube tray and freeze it.

WARNING: <u>If you add oil</u> to your epis, it will keep 4 days in the refrigerator. NEVER leave the mix outside at room temperature. Take what you need and place it back into the refrigerator. If not, it will form a bacterium called botulism that is fatal. It is best to cook your finely cut garlic in oil for 15 min on low. let it cool, then do your epis.

BAK FRITA'

Picture: Chef Gomez by Washington Post

FRY WITH NO SHAME

ACCRAS

This recipe is one of my favorites! just pure roots and spices.
Do not tamper with a tried and true! Accras is like a big hug to your soul!

Servings: 4

60 minutes

Appetizer

ACCRAS WITH TAINO DIP (ACCRAS TAINO)

INGREDIENTS

1 Lb. malanga roots
(white ones, Yautia Blanca)

4 garlic cloves

3 shallots

1 small bunch of parsley

1 small scotch bonnet pepper
or bird pepper (optional)

1 tsp of salt

3 cup Oil for frying

PREP & COOK

1. Clean and peel the malanga roots and grate them finely.
2. In a blender, process all the spices.
3. Incorporate the spices into the grated malanga with a spoon. Make sure everything is mixed.
4. Add the oil to the deep fryer on high heat. When the oil starts to shimmer: Scoop ½ inch-wide strips of malanga mixture with a Tbsp and place in oil.
5. Fry your strips for 2 to 3 minutes or until they reach a golden color.
6. Serve hot with the Taino Dip.

TIPS

As a side dish or part of a finger food platter, this is a great addition to any meal. Crunchy, tasty, and great with pikliz.
I like to let them soak into any meat sauce I have on my plate. I just love these bites!

COW PEAS ACCRAS

ABOUT THIS RECIPE

My cooking journey started with the research of traditional recipes with a story. I wanted to showcase my gastronomic heritage in full. A fact I learned was that 70% of Haïtian household makes accras with malangas/taro. In the North, we have another one we make with cowpeas. This we get from our African ancestors. Whenever we celebrate accras are on the menu.

Servings: 4

60 minutes

Appetizer

COW PEAS ACCRAS (ACCRAS PWA NEG)

INGREDIENTS

- 2 Cups dry Cowpeas
- 2 tbsp of flour
- 1 pinch of ground cloves
- 1 scotch bonnet pepper
- 2 tbsp fresh thyme
- 2 tbsp flat leaves parsley
- 2 tbsp Fresh garlic paste
- 2 tbsp Fresh shallots paste
- 1 medium onion small diced
- 1 red bell pepper small diced
- ¼ cup of vegetable stock
- 1 tbsp of salt or more to taste

FOR FRYING

- 3 tbs palm nut oil and 3 cups vegetable oil

PREP & COOK

1. Soak your peas in water for 2 hours or overnight. Rinse them well.
2. In a food processor, blend the peas with the ground cloves, salt, garlic, shallots, scotch bonnet, parsley, and thyme. Process until smooth.
3. In a bowl, mix the peas preparation with the vegetable stock, flour, onion, and bell peppers. Mix well and set aside.
4. In a heavy pot, on medium-high put the blended oil (palm nut + vegetable oil). Use the back of a table knife to form long strips of the mixture and fry until golden brown.
5. Serve hot.

TIPS

Serve with pikliz on the side. Accras is a great addition to any mixed-finger food platter. Its influence from Africa needs to be highlighted. In Cap-Haitian, we boil the palm nut (Koko Ginen) to extract the red oil. Ginen means Ghana. Our ancestors migrated from there. This recipe is like the Nigerian Akara (bean fritters); ours simply do not have eggs and we keep the skin of the beans on. Nonmatter of its origin, this street food adds a smile on faces, and plates sing in joy!

HERRING PATTIES

ABOUT THIS RECIPE

This is the traditional recipe. You must know that in the '60s, in the northern regions they added calabash. In the '70s, pork sausage patties were made under the Latin influence. In some regions, pikliz is the sole ingredient.

Servings: 4

60 minutes

Appetizer

FRIED HERRING PATTIES (PATE KODE ARAN)

INGREDIENTS

- 5 filets of smoked salted herring
- 2 big shallots or 12 mini ones
- 2 roman tomatoes, seedless, diced
- 1 scotch bonnet pepper
- 1 yellow onion diced

DOUGH

- 2 cups of flour
- 1 cup of water
- 1 tsp of salt
- 2 cups of oil for frying

PREP & COOK

1. Shred the herring & add it to 2 cups of boiled water. Let it sit for 10 minutes, drain and reserve.
2. In a skillet, on medium heat, add 1 tbsp of vegetable oil and cook the tomatoes, onions, shallots, scotch bonnet pepper, and herring for 2 minutes, turn off the heat & taste. Add more pepper if needed, then reserve it.
3. In a bowl, mix in the flour and salt then slowly add water. Knead the dough until it becomes elastic and form a nice ball. Let it rest in a cool area for 1 hour.
4. Lightly flour a flat surface and roll out the dough to ½ centimeter. Cut the dough into circle forms using a pastry cutter. Spoon the herring mix in the center, fold in half. Press the edges with a fork to make dents and close the form.
5. Heat a heavy pot, add 2 cups of oil on medium heat, fry the patties 3 at a time until golden.
6. Serve with pikliz.

TIPS

When in Haïti, you can find these at all hours. Early morning, kids grab them before going to class.

FRIED PLANTAINS

ABOUT THIS RECIPE
I love them with my rice and beans. They also pair well with ratatouille with crab (legim ak crab).

Please visit www.chefsmanifesto.com

Servings: 2

15 minutes

Appetizer

FRIED PLANTAINS (BANNANN FRI)

INGREDIENTS

- 2 green plantains
- Juice of 1 sour orange
- 1 cup of water
- Salt to taste

- 2 cups oil for frying

PREP & COOK

1. Peel and cut each plantain into 4 diagonal pieces and place in a bowl large enough.
2. Heat a skillet on medium heat; pour the vegetable oil.
3. Fry the plantains until golden in color; 4 minutes in total.
4. Remove and flatten to ½ inch approximately (use a Tostonera or the back of a small plate).
5. In a bowl put 1 cup of water, sour orange juice & salt.
6. Dip each plantain in the seasoned water for a few seconds and fry again until crisp.

TIPS

Great eaten alone with Pikliz as an appetizer. Or served with fried fish or any other fried or meat in a savory tomato sauce.

To have a nice Fritay platter: Slice some breadfruit and follow steps 5 to 6. Skin and slice in julienne or batonnet some sweet potatoes. Or you can also cut them in rounds of ¼ inches thick. Fry them until a nice crust forms but the center remains a bit soft. (5 minutes approximately).

CHICKEN FRITTERS

ABOUT THIS RECIPE

During communion (Eucharist) season in Haïti; this appetizer is served at the receptions. The legendary band Bossa Combo has a famous song, which immortalizes this recipe. This is how serious we take our chicken fritters. Immortalize this recipe.

Servings: 2

30 minutes

Appetizer

CHICKEN FRITTERS (MARINAD POUL)

INGREDIENTS

1 chicken, cooked, deboned, and cut into small pieces

1 big shallot or 5 small ones

1 whole scotch bonnet pepper

6 cloves of garlic

½ tsp of ground cloves

¼ cup of parsley with sprigs

1 tbsp of salt

2 cups of flour

1 tbsp fresh thyme leaves

1 onion brunoise cut

1 ½ cup of water (or chicken water/stock)

1 tsp of baking soda

Vegetable oil to fry

PREP & COOK

1. Blend the spices until they form a fine paste.
2. In a big bowl whisk the flour and baking soda; add the spices mix, fresh thyme, onions, and water then mix to form a smooth batter.
3. Add the cut chicken. You might need to adjust the batter; it needs to remain smooth (like pancake mix). At this point, add more of the chicken stock leftover from cooking, or plain water. I prefer the leftover chicken stock to make the batter. It adds more flavor.
4. Use a small ladder to drop the batter into your hot frying oil. One after the other. But not too many at once. They need enough space to turn while they get a golden color.
5. Once golden, remove from oil onto paper towels on a plate to capture the dripping oil. Serve hot!

TIPS

In some towns, they add smoked herrings and tomatoes.
This marinade base can be used with either shrimp or lobster.
There is another recipe for "morue" Cod fritters. We use boiled and mashed breadfruit or mashed potatoes instead of the flour base.

FRIED CHICKEN

Chicken is widely consumed in Haiti. While classical cooking techniques do not recommend washing chicken for cross-contamination, in the Caribbean we do.

Servings: 4

60 minutes

Appetizer

FRIED CHICKEN (POUL FRI)

INGREDIENTS

- 2 lbs chicken drumstick
- 3 limes
- 2 tablespoon of white vinegar
- 1 sour orange
- 1 tsp of salt
- 1 cube of chicken bouillon
- 1 bunch of fresh flat-leaf parsley
- 1 whole head of garlic
- 1 scotch bonnet pepper
- 4 sprigs of fresh thyme
- Flour for coating
- 2 cup Oil for frying

*MARINATE

Mix your epis blend with the cube of chicken bouillon. Add the juice of the sour orange and the rest of the lime. Add the salt, thyme & mix well

PREP & COOK

1. Put the chicken in a clean bowl.
2. Pour the white vinegar on the meat and the juice of 2 limes. Rub the limes over the skin. Rinse with cold water, drain, and reserve.
3. Boil 3 cups of water. Press the juice of half a lime in the water. Let it boil and pour over the chicken. Let it soak for 1 or 2 minutes this will help remove any yellow skin attach to the end of the drumstick. Drain the water. Your chicken is ready to receive your epis blend*.
4. Marinate the chicken in the fridge for 2-3 hours or overnight.
5. Remove the chicken from the fridge 30 minutes before cooking. In a pan boil your chicken with 1 cup of warm water for 30 minutes.
6. Heat the oil in a skillet, coat the pieces of chicken with the flour and fry for 8-10 minutes or until golden.

TIPS

Using vinegar, lime, and hot water helps to kill some bacteria.
Eating meat in the Caribbean is very safe and rare are cases of food poisoning.
In our culture, this is a traditional way to clean and cook meat.

FRIED KASHKI FISH

ABOUT THIS RECIPE

Fried Kachki is eaten as is, with cassava or Bannann peze. A hot shallot sauce* is a great sauce to go with these delicious bites.

You can replace the pisket with soft shell crabs, any other cuts of fish, oyster, shrimp, or mushrooms for vegetarians.

Servings: 4-6

20-25 minutes

Appetizer

FRIED KACHKI FISH (PISKET FRI)

INGREDIENTS

1 lb. Kachki fish

1 red onion minced

1 tsp sea salt

1 fresh Curcuma finger grated or 2 tbs of Curcuma powder

2 green onions minced

1 scotch bonnet pepper minced

1 small green bell pepper minced

1 cup of flour

½ cup of water

Juice of 1 lime

2 cup Oil for frying

PREP & COOK

1. In a bowl, mix in the flour & water.
2. Clean the fish in a colander under running water. Set it aside to drain.
3. Mince the onion, green onions, scotch bonnet, green bell pepper as finely as possible.
4. in a bowl large enough to receive all the ingredients: First, rub the fish with salt & lime juice. Second, add the minced ingredients and the flour batter. Mix everything well.
5. In a deep-frying pot, on medium heat, add your oil. When ready:
6. Fry one Tbsp of fish batter until golden. Taste to adjust seasoning.
7. Fry your batter to a golden color.
8. Remove from oil and place on paper towels to drain excess oil.

TIPS

Shallot sauce: In a small pot, on high heat, add 2 tbsp of oil. Add a handful of shallots roughly diced. Turn off the heat. Add 3 small, diced scotch bonnet peppers with seeds, a pinch of salt, and a Tbsp of sour orange juice. Your sauce is ready.

If you cannot find Kachki fish, use smelt fishes or small anchovies.

FRIED FISH

ABOUT THIS RECIPE

Granny Cienne and her best friend used to bring us, kids, to Labadee village on weekends. While camping there once, I ate the best bouillon pêcheur! However, their seaside fried fish is top-notch. Trust me.

Servings: 4

40 minutes

Entree

LABADEE BEACH'S FRIED FISH (PWASON FRI LABADEE)

INGREDIENTS

- 2 parrot Fish (pwason Boutou)
- 1 ½ of salt
- ½ green scotch bonnet pepper
- 4 cloves of garlic
- ½ cup of white flour
- 4 Limes
- 1 cup oil for frying

PREP & COOK

1. Use a knife or a spoon to remove any scales, work from tail to head.
2. If there are still fish innards remove them. Remove any dark membranes and the dorsal fin. Rinse the fish rapidly in cold water. Put the fish in a clean bowl.
3. Cut 3 limes in half; use the juice and lime skins to clean the fish again. Rinse well.
4. On a cutting board, place the fish and do two slashes on the diagonal along the body, on both sides, it will help the seasoning to flavor the fish and it will cook faster as well.
5. Make a spice paste with garlic, salt, and scotch bonnet.
6. Marinate the fish in a bowl with that paste and add the juice of the remaining lime for 1 or 2 hours.
7. In a skillet, heat oil, lightly dust the fish with flour. Grip the fish by the tail with a tong. Carefully lower it in the oil headfirst. Fry each side for 4 minutes. Eat with Bannann Peze or Cassava bread.

TIPS

Seaside grilled fish: steps 1&2, soak the fish in a bowl with seawater (10 min.) Steps 3 to 6 (salt to taste). Oil your <u>hot</u> grill and cook the fish.

Our version of paella: In a flavorful broth, add rice & veggies. Top it off with seasoned fish. Cook as usual.

FRIED FRESHWATER FISH

This is a typical dish of "Haut du Cap". A section outside the town of Cap-Haïtien. The "Kabo", a freshwater fish, is a small club-shaped type sensitive to water pollution. its presence is an excellent indicator of the cleanliness of the place. Usually found in the Northern part of Haiti, especially in Haut du Cap. A few days of rain will bring an abundance of Kabo.

Servings: 4

60 minutes

Entree

FRIED FRESHWATER FISH (KABO FRI)

INGREDIENTS

2 lb small "kabo" or any small freshwater fish

1 cup white flour

1 tbsp of garlic paste

4 bird peppers

1 tsp ground black pepper

2 tbsp salt

2 tbsp lime juice + 3 whole lime

OIl for frying

PREP & COOK

1. Clean your fish and use the 3 limes cut into quarters to gently rub the lime and its juice on the inside and skin of the fish, rinse well, pat dry, and reserve.
2. Mix the garlic paste, bird peppers, 2 tbsp of lime juice, and the salt.
3. Marinate the fishes in that mixture.
4. In a bowl combine the flour and the black pepper and mix.
5. Dip each fish into the flour mixture, then fry until golden and crispy. Serve hot!

TIPS

Substitute the kabo with any small freshwater fish that you find in your fish market. You can also cook the freshwater fish in a creole sauce and serve it with white rice.

FRIED OCTOPUS

ABOUT THIS RECIPE
If you can get cleaned octopus from the fish market it is a time saver. However, you can always choose to clean the octopus yourself.

Servings: 4

3:40 minutes

Entree

FRIED OCTOPUS (CHATWOUJ FRI)

INGREDIENTS

- 2 medium octopus cleaned
- A few sprigs of fresh thyme
- fresh oregano
- 1 tbsp fresh thick leaf thyme or
- Lemon balm leaves
- 1 tbsp fresh basil leaves
- 1 bunch of parsley
- 2 whole leeks cut in 2
- Salt to taste
- 1 tbsp whole black pepper
- 1 scotch bonnet pepper
- Juice of 1 sour orange
- 1 head of garlic just peel them
- 2 big shallots

- 1 cup Oil for frying

PREP & COOK

1. On high heat, use a big pot and add 3 quarts of water, the parsley with sprigs attach, the thyme, oregano, thick leaf thyme, basil, black pepper, garlic, and leek. Bring to a boil.
2. Using kitchen tongs, dip the cleaned octopus 4 or 5 times into the boiling water. Turn the heat to low and let the octopus simmer for one hour. Add 15mn if not completely tender. 10 minutes before the end of the cooking add the juice of the sour orange and cook the octopus for 1h30 minutes.
3. Blend the shallots and scotch bonnet pepper and salt to taste.
4. Remove the octopus from the cooking liquid, cut it into bite pieces and marinate with the spices blend for 20 to 30 minutes.
5. Heat your oil and fry.
6. Once fried, sprinkle with sour orange juice or lime juice. Serve hot

TIPS
A simpler way to enjoy grilled octopus is to pour over it a sauce made of garlic, parsley, lemon, and butter.

FRIED LOBSTER

ABOUT THIS RECIPE

This recipe is from the beach area called Gelee. This marvelous place is after Les Cayes in the south of Haiti.

Gelee is famous for its fried lobster.

Servings: 4

20-25 minutes

Entree

GELEE'S FRIED LOBSTER (OMA FRI LANME GELEE)

INGREDIENTS

- 2 pounds lobster tails in shell
- ½ tsp Roucou (annatto powder)
- ½ cup white flour
- 4 cloves of garlic
- 1 small yellow onion
- ½ tsp of Sea Salt
- Juice of 3 limes
- ½ green scotch bonnet pepper
- Parsley for garnish

1/2 cup oil for frying.

If using a deep fryer, turn the heat on 350to 375.

Garnish your lobster plate with a few lemon/ lime quarters.

PREP & COOK

1. Use a sharp knife to cut off the lobster tail flippers. Put your finger through the hole it created and push the meat out the other end. OR, cut the shells with scissors or a sharp knife. Peel off the shell and remove the meat.
2. Remove the intestinal tract and throw it away. Then, rinse the lobsters in cool water and drain.
3. Blend the garlic and onion and green scotch bonnet, add the salt.
4. Coat the lobster tails with the spice blend. Roll them in the flour mixed with the roucou and set aside.
5. In a skillet, heat the vegetable oil on medium-high heat, shake the lobster to remove any excess flour, fry for 3-4 min.
6. Squeeze lime juice right away on the lobster. Garnish with parsley.
7. Serve hot.

TIPS

You can substitute the lobster with Jumbo shrimps, or regular size shrimps.
For visual effect, fry the lobster with the shell on.
Use the lobster shells to make a seafood stock/broth. (If not right away, freeze them).

FRIED PORK

Growing up in Cap-Haitian, I would seem partial to its people's cooking. However, this meal requires a few small steps that make all the difference between yesterday's and today's quick, shortcut way of cooking! The "yesterdays" were all about quality and taste and freshness; I add to that fun and passion!

Servings: 6

60 minutes

Entree

CAP-HAÏTIEN FRIED PORK (GRIOT OKAP)

INGREDIENTS

- 2 pounds pork shoulder/ skin on
- 5 fresh basil leaves
- 1/2 cup sour orange
- 1/4 cup of Caribbean dark rhum
- 1 green scotch bonnet pepper
- 1 tsp of sea salt
- 1 small bunch of flat-leaf parsley
- 8 cups of water

- 2 cup Oil for frying

PREP & COOK

1. Rinse and clean the meat and cut into medium size chunks.
2. Marinate overnight or 2 hours before cooking with the salt, basil leaves, sour orange juice, and rhum.
3. Put the meat in an 8-quart pot and cook on medium heat, uncovered, for 5 minutes.
4. Add the water and parsley. Boil on low heat until meat is fork-tender.
5. Mid cooking adjusts the salt to taste If necessary.
6. Fry the pieces of pork in a fryer or heavy pot until golden brown and skin crispy.

TIPS

Serve with fried plantains or Haïtian National rice (rice and peas) with pikliz.

Griot is also great on a platter along with fried octopus, plantain, breadfruit, accras, fish, marinade, and others of your liking.

From the marinated pork, you can make "Tatouni". Boil the pork, add lots of thyme, more roucou sauce or tomato paste, and onions... voila! "Ragout de Porc". Eat it with boiled green plantains and yams.

FRIED FRESHWATER FISH

EXTRA STREET FOODS

SCRAMBLED EGGS WITH OYSTERS

ABOUT THIS RECIPE

Aquin is the only town in Haiti known for that recipe.

Oysters are best in the colder months from September to April. They reproduce in the summer.

Servings: 3

20 minutes

Entree

SCRAMBLED EGGS WITH OYSTERS FROM AQUIN

INGREDIENTS

8 fresh shuck oysters

3 eggs

1 Seedless scotch bonnet pepper

1 tsp parsley for garnishing

1 sprig of chive, chopped thin

1 tbsp of shallots, chopped

Salt to taste

2 tbsp of vegetable oil

PREP & COOK

1. Remove the oysters from the shells and rinse to remove any grainy particles or pieces of shells. Strain and pat dry.
2. In a bowl, mix the minced scotch bonnet, chopped chive, and the oysters and reserve.
3. In another bowl, whisk the eggs with the salt and reserve.
4. In a frying pan on medium-high, put the oil, wait 30 seconds. Add the chopped shallots. Lower the heat and add the egg mixture and quickly scramble it.
5. Within a minute, add the oysters and let them cook for 1 minute.
6. Sprinkle the chopped parsley on top before serving hot.

TIPS

Some people like it also with tomatoes and a dash of garlic.
Oysters should smell fresh. You can also store your oysters in the refrigerator in a closed container or sealed plastic bag. They will keep fresh like this for 1-2 weeks after harvest.
Presentation: Serve on a bed of ice or coarse salt with lemon/ lime wedges.

BOILED BREADFRUI

ABOUT THIS RECIPE

The Tainos cooked the "Lame" or Breadfruit underground. They cut open the head of the fruit, removed some of the flesh, and added coconut milk with fresh fish, annatto seeds, and scotch bonnet leaves. Closing it back with the head, placed it on hot coals; Covering it with leaves and dirt to cook.

Nowadays, breadfruit was cooked with smoked herring, tomatoes, scotch bonnet, and shallots the same way!

Servings: 2

40 minutes

Entree

BOILED BREADFRUIT (LAM BOUYI)

INGREDIENTS

- 1 Breadfruit
- Salt

PREP & COOK

1. Make the Creamy coconut sauce (Vinèg lèt) found in the 1st section.
2. Cut the breadfruit into 4 big slices. With a sharp knife, remove the skin. It is a bit tough, so be careful not to cut yourself.
3. Put the cleaned slices in a pot big enough and cover them with water, add the salt and cook for 15 min.
4. When the breadfruit is tender, remove it from heat and water.
5. Dice the slices and plate them as you wish, add the sauce, and enjoy!

TIPS

Lam can also be thinly sliced and fried the same way as plantain.
"Lame Fri" or fried breadfruit is eaten with "piman konfi".

HAÏTIAN NATIONAL RIC[E]

ABOUT THIS RECIPE

Chodye in Kreyol is like the caldero fondido used in Latin America. Using a chodye will give the perfect "gratin"(scorched rice) at the bottom of the pan.

Bacon or enduit can be omitted for a 100% plant-based dish.

Servings: 6

60+45 minutes

Entree

HAITIAN NATIONAL RICE (DIRI PWA KOLE)

INGREDIENTS

FOR THE BEANS

4 oz dry red kidney beans

8 cups of water

FOR THE RICE

2 cups parboiled long grain rice

½ cup enduit or salted pork or bacon roughly chopped

1 tsp freshly ground black pepper

1 tsp salt

Spices blend of 6 cloves of garlic, 1 shallot, 2 tbsp of minced fresh flat-leaf parsley

3 sprigs of thyme

1 green scotch bonnet pepper

3 whole cloves or ¼ Tsp clove powder

¼ cup of vegetable oil, or Annatto oil.

1 tbsp butter (optional)

PREP & COOK

1. Rinse the beans. In their cooking pot cover them with water with a pinch of bicarbonate overnight.
2. Remove the overnight water, add 8 fresh cups of water, and bring to a boil. Cook until tender but still firm to the touch.
3. Strain the beans and reserve the cooking liquid.
4. In a "Chodye" heat the oil over medium-high & sauté the beans & the bacon until they are crispy. Add the spices blend, salt, and thyme. Cook for 1 minute. Add 3 ¼ cups of the bean water. Bring to a boil.
5. Rinse the rice in cool water to remove the starch, drain. Add it to the boiling water and stir.
6. Adjust the seasoning and add the whole pepper and the clove powder.
7. Lower the heat to medium-low. Cook until the water is not seen on the surface. Add the butter.
8. Reduce heat to the lowest and cover tightly with a lid.
9. Cook for another 18-20 minutes.
10. Fluff and serve!

TIPS

Bacon or enduit can be omitted for a 100% plant-based dish.

SPICY COW COD SOU

ABOUT THIS RECIPE
Janjol is considered an aphrodisiac and it is a very spicy soup.

Servings: 6

60 minutes

Entree

SPICY COW COD SOUP (JANJOL OR BEGA)

INGREDIENTS

- 1 cleaned Cow Cod diced
- ½ lb. torched cow foot without the bones cut in small pieces.
- 1 cup fresh green peas or lima beans soaked overnight
- 2 cups of homemade tomato sauce or 1 jar (16 oz) RAGÚ® with roasted garlic and vegetable or 2 (8oz) V8 vegetable
- 3 sprigs of thyme
- 2 scallions diced small
- 3 whole cloves
- 4 tbsp of epis blend
- 2 scotch bonnet pepper
- 2 tbsp dark rum
- 3 homemade bouillon cubes
- Juice of 1 lime
- 2 medium carrots diced small
- 2 yautia (malanga) diced small
- 1 whole yellow onion
- 1 tbsp vegetable oil
- Marinate the Cow cord and Cow foot skin in the epis blend with the scotch bonnets overnight.

PREP & COOK

1. In a pressure cooker, heat the oil and saute the scallions; add the thyme and cloves. Then add the cow skin and cow cord. Keep cooking for 4 minutes while adding continuously ¼ cup of water and scraping the bottom of the cooker. Deglaze with the dark rum.
2. Add 4 cups of water. Cover the pressure cooker for 25mins. Check if it is tender. If not, add 2 more cups of hot water and cook for 10 more minutes. Remove the cloves and discard. Transfer everything else to a bigger pot and reserve.
3. Sift the flour in a bowl, add salt, pepper, oil, and water. Knead your dough and form dumplings the size of your little finger.
4. In a pot, add 10 cups of water, the green peas, carrots, yautia, 3 cubes of vegetable stock, 1 whole onion. Cook for 5 minutes then add the dumplings and cook for 5 more minutes. Discard the onion.
5. Transfer the cooked vegetables to the pot with the cow cord, add the RAGÚ® sauce. Let it simmer on low heat for 3-5 minutes. Rectify your seasoning, add the lime juice. Serve Hot!

SAUTÉED WHELK

ABOUT THIS RECIPE
Brigot or Bourgot in french, also known as **whelk. Whelks** are large marine **snails** (gastropods) with spiral shells. A variety, known as the dogwhelk, can be used to produce red-purple and violet dyes.

Servings: 2

30 minutes

Entree

SAUTÉED WHELKS (BRIGOT OU BOURGOT)

INGREDIENTS

3 Lbs. brigot with shells

1 tsp black pepper

1 tbsp Salt

6 cloves of garlic germ removed

1 small red onion diced

½ lime

Olive oil

SEASONED BUTTER

8 oz soft unsalted butter

½ bunch flat-leaf parsley

1 tsp pink peppercorn

In a food processor, mince the garlic, peppercorn, and parsley. Add the soft butter and mix well.

PREP & COOK

1. With the shells on, rinse the brigot and brush to remove any algae or sand. Leave in water for a few hours.
2. In a large pot add the brigot, cover with water, and add the salt and pepper. Bring to a boil and let it cook for 10 minutes (do not overcook or it will be rubbery).
3. Turn off the heat, cover the pot, and let stand for 5 minutes.
4. Using tongs, remove from the water. With a clean towel, hold the brigot and remove it from the shell. Remove the tough covering and the dark membrane, rinse the meat using the cooking water.
5. Thinly slice your brigot.
6. Heat a skillet, add 1 tbsp of oil. Fry the onions for 2 minutes, add the seasoned butter cook for 1 minute then add the brigot. Sauté for 1 minute. Add scotch bonnet pepper to taste. Pour lime juice before serving.

TIPS

For a gourmet touch, white wine can be added instead of lime juice.

Brigot can be grilled as well and can be cooked with Haïtian epis.

GRILLED CONC

ABOUT THIS RECIPE
There is never a time where you are at the beach and you do not crave these bites. Either with or without the hot sauce. Just load it with lemon slices and I am good to go!

Servings: 4

30 minutes

Entree

GRILLED CONCH (LAMBI GRIYE)

INGREDIENTS
4 pounds Fresh Conch in their shell

FOR THE HOT SAUCE
4 sour oranges

1 lime

1 clove of garlic

8 scotch bonnet pepper cut in half

1 tbsp of sea salt

1 Bottle to store the hot sauce

Clean your conch shells thoroughly and leave them in water to remove most of the sand inside the shells.

PREP & COOK

A week before.

a. Rinse and wipe dry the scotch bonnet pepper, cut them in half, and put them in the bottle.
b. Pour the citrus juices, the salt, and the garlic clove (whole) over the peppers. Shake well and reserve.

1. On a hot grill, layer the conchs while they are still in the shells.
2. When cooking they will start to bubble while releasing water. Cook for 7-10 minutes.
3. Remove from the shells, remove the hard covering and intestines.
4. Rinse in warm water.
5. You can serve them whole or cut in thin slices, pour the hot sauce over the cooked conch, and enjoy!

TIPS
This method of cooking can only be used with fresh conch.

KACHKI IN CREOLE SAUC

Pisket is a small silvery fish of the anchovy family. They feed on plankton and move in schools with perfectly coordinated movements. They are found near the coast, in dark areas, near caves, or overhangs.

A meal much appreciated by the Trevally, Thazards, Pelicans, and humans. Size 4/7 cm

Servings: 4

30 minutes

Entree

KACHKI IN CREOLE SAUCE (PISKET NAN SÒS)

INGREDIENTS

2 lbs Kachki fish

Juice of 2 limes

2 tbsp of tomato paste

1 onion cut into rings

3 sprigs of fresh thyme

1 cups of hot water

3 Tbsp of vegetable oil

SPICE(EPIS) BLEND

3 cloves of garlic,

1 tbsp of salt

3 Tbsp of fresh parsley

half of the lime juice

1 scotch bonnet pepper

1 green onion

PREP & COOK

1. Place the fish in a colander and rinse under running water twice.
2. In a big bowl with cold water add half of the lime juice, add the small fish, and let soak for 2 minutes. Drain the water.
3. In a skillet, heat the oil with the tomato paste, add the onions, and epis blend. Cook for 1 minute on high heat.
4. Lower the heat and add the fish and the rest of the lime juice. Add the thyme cover and cook for 5 minutes. Add 1 cup of hot water and cook for 10 more minutes.
5. Taste and adjust seasoning before serving. Enjoy!

TIPS

Pisket is a small white fish that is delicious cooked in a creole sauce or fried.
Pisket is eaten with white rice or rice with pigeon peas.
Cassava bread (kasav) is a great option.

SAUTÉED CURED GOAT

ABOUT THIS RECIPE

The Tainos invented the BBQ. Not today's BBQ grill as we know it. They would wrap the meat in banana leaves cooked over coils and sometimes covered deep in a hole with rocks and more coils.

As culinary writer Aralyn Beaumont writes in her essay *Leaves Make things Steamy*, "Cooking in leaves is one of humanity's simplest and most elegant culinary ideas. Its ubiquity unites us. The myriad ways we adapt the same basic principle is what makes food interesting."

Servings: 2

30 minutes

Entree

SAUTÉED CURED GOAT (SESIN KABRIT)

INGREDIENTS

3lbs <u>pre-cured goat meat</u> (sesin)

2 small onions, sliced

5 small shallots, chopped

7 cloves of garlic, chopped

3 Tbsp of fresh parsley

2 sprigs of thyme

3 Tbsp of vegetable oil.

Juice of 1 lime

PREP & COOK

1. *The day before* cooking your sesin, in a big bowl, add the meat (about 3 pounds after curing) and at least 10 cups of cold water and leave it in the fridge. (min, 6 hours).
2. In a large pot, place your goat meat, add the thyme, parsley, and garlic. Cover with water and cook until tender. If necessary, add water.
3. Remove the meat from the cooking liquid.
4. In a frying pan, heat the oil. Add the meat, shallots, onions, and lime juice. Let it cook for 2 minutes.
5. Serve hot with cassava bread or fried plantain.

TIPS

When goat was introduced in North America there was no way to preserve it. They would cut it in pieces, add fair amount of salt and sun dried them. That method for goat is called "SESIN". With this process, meat can take 4 to 5 days to dry/cure.

Sesin can also be eaten grilled with cassava bread.

The method of using sour orange juice and salt for curing meat is also named "Saumur".

HAÏTIAN BEEF POTAG

ABOUT THIS RECIPE
We love our Beef potage. Our grandmothers used to have this ready for our traveling relatives. A warm welcome after a long trip!

This recipe is quite long to follow, but fret not for you will have a belly full of goodness. Enjoy with your family and friends.

Servings: 6-8

2:45 minutes

Entree

HAÏTIAN BEEF POTAGE (BOUYON BÈF)

INGREDIENTS

FOR THE MEAT

1 lb. Beef shank +1 bone marrow

Spices blend of 3 shallots, 5 cloves of garlic, 2 tbsp of parsley, 2 green onions, 1 tsp salt

5 cloves

1 tsp of paprika

2 sour oranges juice

1 lime juice

3 cup unsalted beef stock

2 cups of water

1 tsp of oil

FOR THE POTAGE

2 carrots roughly chopped

3 malanga roots roughly chopped

1 yellow yam cut in big cubes

1 white yam cut in big cubes

1 green plantain cut into 4 pieces

10 cups of water

1 quart of vegetable stock (unsalted)

2 sprigs of fresh thyme

1 cup spinach

1/2 cup watercress

1 tbsp of tomato paste

1/2 tsp of lime juice

FOR THE DUMPLINGS

PREP & COOK

1. Cut the meat into ½ inch cubes, clean & marinate with the blend of spices, sour oranges, and limes juice. refrigerate for one hour or more.
2. Remove from the fridge 30 minutes before cooking.
3. In a soup pot over high medium heat; add the oil, the bone marrow & let cook until the fat starts melting, now add the meat and brown it.
4. Add the paprika and deglaze with beef stock and water. Cover the pot loosely with its lid. Reduce heat to low and let simmer for 45 min. or until meat is tender.
5. When ready, remove the meat & leave the fat that remains on the bottom.
6. Add the malanga, yams, and plantain and sauté for 2 minutes.
7. Add the tomato paste and thyme; cook for another minute and pour the vegetable stock and water; let boil for 15 minutes on medium heat.
8. Remove the thyme & add the meat back to the pot. Now add the carrots and the dumplings*. Cook for another 10 minutes. Skim the fat on top of the potage. Let It cook on low heat for another 5 minutes.
9. 3 minutes before serving, add the watercress, spinach, and lime juice.
10. Taste for salt and adjust.
11. Serve hot.

1 cup all-purpose flour

1/2 tsp of salt

1/4 cup of vegetable stock

2 tbsp of water

1 tsp freshly ground black pepper

1 tbsp vegetable oil

*Mix the salt, water, stock, ground pepper, and oil in a bowl. Now add the flour and mix to form a soft dough; knead for 1 or 2 minutes. Form medium (lime size) size balls of dough or Index(finger) long shaped.

TIPS

For a thicker potage, make a slurry of 1 tbsp of cornstarch to 1 tbsp of cold water and add it to the soup 2 minutes before serving.

SWEET TREATS

STEAMED CORNMEAL PUDDING

Pudding Ablin also called Akassan Fey cooked is eaten with cane syrup. Akasan is a breakfast made with cornmeal cook in milk like rice flour. Akasan Fey has a thicker consistency and is a dessert.

Servings: 4-6

45 minutes

Dessert

STEAMED CORNMEAL PUDDING (ABLIN/ AKASAN FEY)

INGREDIENTS
¾ cup of fine yellow cornmeal

1 cup of water

1 cup of evaporated milk

½ cup of coconut milk

1 lime peel

3-star anise

1 pinch of salt

1 tsp ground cinnamon

1 tsp ground nutmeg

1 tbsp vanilla extract

1 tbsp of butter

Dark Cane syrup

Banana leaves or aluminum foil.

If you are using the leaves, cut them into 5-inch squares and boil them to soften them.

If not, cut your aluminum foil.

PREP & COOK
1. In a saucepan on medium heat, add the water, lime peel, star anise, cinnamon, and nutmeg. Bring to a boil. Now remove and discard the star anise and the lime peel.
2. Lower the heat and slowly whisk in the cornmeal. Add the evaporated milk and the coconut milk in a slow pour while still whisking.
3. Keep whisking until the mixture thickens. Turn off the heat.
4. Finish up by adding the vanilla extract and salt and set aside to cool.
5. In your leaves, add a scoop of mixture in the center. Fold the left, then right sides over, then fold the top and bottom parts.
6. Tie the leaves with the baker's twine. You do not need the twine for the foil.
7. In a pot, bring water to a boil. Add your wrapped packages and reduce the heat to low. Cook for 35 minutes with the lid on.

TIPS
I prefer steamed to boiled. For this, use a "round rack" to place inside your pot. The water should stay under the leaves or aluminum packages.

RUSTIC COCONUT COOKIE

A true Taino recipe adapted through the years. Originally, coconut was shredded and grilled, they would then add water, coconut milk, and cassava flour.

A delicious, sweet treat full of flavors and a great addition to those wonderful afternoon treats that we used to have at teatime.

Servings: 12

40 minutes

Dessert

RUSTIC COCONUT COOKIES (KOKONET)

INGREDIENTS

1 cup sweetened grated coconut

1 lb white flour

2 eggs

½ cup of white granulated sugar

1 tbsp baking powder

1 tsp butter

1 tsp ground cinnamon

1 tsp ground nutmeg

1 tsp white vanilla

PREP & COOK

1. Preheat the oven to 350.
2. Oil a cookie sheet.
3. In a bowl, thoroughly mix all the ingredients.
4. With an ice cream scoop, form small balls of the dough.
5. Arrange the coconut balls mixture onto the cookie sheet and cook until golden.

TIPS

We drink them with a hot beverage like hot milk chocolate with whipped cream.
You can use freshly grated coconut instead of the store-bought. However, you must increase the sugar amount by ¼ cup.

GRANNY CIENNE BUTTER COOKIES

ABOUT THIS RECIPE
I learned this recipe when I was young. Always hanging at my grandma's apron. This is a cookie you need to have at hand for everything life throws at you!

Servings: 12

40 minutes

Dessert

GRANNY CIENNE BUTTER COOKIES

INGREDIENTS

1 cup of butter or 8 oz

2 ½ cup of flour

2 eggs

½ tsp salt

1 tbsp of vanilla extract

Zest of 2 limes

PREP & COOK

1. Preheat the oven to 350.
2. In a medium-size bowl, sift the flour, add the salt, and stir. Reserve.
3. Cream the butter and sugar with a hand mixer until light and fluffy.
4. Beat in the eggs one at a time and add the zest of the limes.
5. Add the vanilla extract and continue to mix until well combined.
6. Gradually add the flour until the flour is mixed in. Do not over-mix.
7. At this point, you can cover the dough and refrigerate or use it right away. Fill your cookie press and form your cookies onto an ungreased cookie sheet.
8. Bake until golden on the edges. 8-10 min.
9. Lay the cookies on a cooling rack; save them into an airtight container to keep them fresh and crispy.

TIPS

Chilling the dough one or 2 hours before pressing them on the cookie sheet will prevent the cookies from spreading too much while cooking. They will maintain their pattern. Depending on the cookie press pattern, you can add dry raisins or cherries to the center of the cookies before baking them.

COCONUT FUDG

A sweet finale to a Caribbean meal. No trip to the beach is complete without those. Have them with a fresh glass of coconut water after a wonderful grilled lobster... sweet life!

Servings: 12

40-50 minutes

Dessert

COCONUT FUDGE (DOUS KOKOYE)

INGREDIENTS

1 cup of coconut milk

1 cup evaporated milk

4 cups of brown sugar

1 tsp ground nutmeg

Pinch of salt

IF you like the texture, add ¼ cup of shredded coconut.

PREP & COOK

1. In a pot, mix all the ingredients until the sugar is dissolved.
2. Bring to a boil on low heat.
3. Stir frequently until it forms a paste.
4. On an oiled cookie sheet or use parchment paper, pour in the mixture, and flatten it at about half an inch high.
5. Let cool for several hours. Cut in squares or diagonals and serve.

TIPS

If you leave the milk and sugar mixture unattended, it will rise and spoil your oven. Or you might burn the fudge.
This is a labor of love. Take this time to reflect or plan other recipes from this book. But keep an eye on your fudge!

HAÏTIAN DUKUNU

ABOUT THIS RECIPE
This recipe comes from the Garifuna (African/Amerindians). They lived in the north along the coasts. A more detailed story in Extra Tips

Servings: 4-6

30 minutes

Dessert

HAÏTIAN DUKUNU (DUKUNU)

INGREDIENTS

¼ cup sweet, grated coconut

1 cup of coconut milk

1 cup evaporated milk

½ cup of water

1 cup grated sweet potatoes (white flesh, red skin)

½ cup cornflour

Zest of one lime

½ teaspoon of cinnamon, nutmeg,

1 tbsp of vanilla extract

1 pinch of salt

Banana leaves or aluminum foil

Bakers twine

If you are using the leaves, cut them into 5-inch squares and boil them to soften them.

If not, cut your aluminum foil.

PREP & COOK

1. In a saucepan on low heat, add the water, lime zest, and the grated sweet potatoes. Bring to a boil and cook for 2 minutes.
2. Add the evaporated milk and the coconut milk. Lower the heat and slowly whisk in the cornflour.
3. Keep mixing with your spoon until the mixture starts to thicken. Add the nutmeg, cinnamon, and vanilla extract. Now add the sugar and grated coconut. Let cook on low heat until it forms a loose paste. Remove from heat and let it cool down.
4. In your leaves, add a scoop of mixture in the center. Fold the left, then right sides over, then fold the top and bottom parts.
5. Tie the leaves with the baker's twine.
6. In a pot, bring water to a boil. Add your wrapped packages and reduce the heat to low. Cook for 35 minutes with the lid on.
7. Serve it with rhum raisin molasses sauce.

TIPS

prefer steamed to boiled. For this, use a round rack.

With the addition of the Molasses sauce, this recipe is a prelude to the next cookbook of our *New Haïtian and Caribbean Gastronomy* series.

MILK CHEESE & CURDLED MILK

ABOUT THIS RECIPE

My mother loves curdled milk... I never did. However, give me that cheese with the rhum raisin syrup and I am good for days! This recipe celebrates our French gastronomy heritage. "Fromage blanc" is a fresh cheese originating from the north of France. In Benin, Africa, their "Lait Caillé" uses this curdled milk recipe as a base.

MILK CHEESE & CURDLED MILK (FROMAJ LÈT AK LÈT KAYE)

INGREDIENTS

1 gallon of milk (unpasteurized), or Fresh milk (if accessible)

Half a lime/ Cheesecloth/ Rhum raisin & Molasses sauce

THE MAKING OF CURDLED MILK

1. Curdled milk is the first process in cheese making. The coagulation can be caused by adding rennet or any edible acidic substance such as lemon juice or vinegar.
2. Fresh milk is mostly used uncooked, but we recommend heating the milk on medium-low for 1-2 min. *(DO NOT BOIL)* to remove any bacteria. It should be warm.
3. Turn off the heat and add the lime juice *(lime juice is omitted in the traditional recipe and we do not heat the milk).*
4. Let cool at room temperature overnight. The lime juice will help in forming the curd. The curd will shrink and separate a little from the milk water (the whey).
5. You have made *"Lèt Kaye"*. Refrigerate for up to 1 hour and enjoy with white sugar or cane syrup.

THE MAKING OF MILK CHEESE

1. Follow steps 1 to 4. Do not shake or stir it.
2. Skim the heavy cream on top of the milk. *(You can make homemade butter with it or discard it).*
3. Put a cheesecloth or a muslin on top of a bowl. Pour the curds and the liquid, thus separating the curd from the whey *(milk water)*. *(back in the days they used a clean pillowcase with a metal wire hanged on a pantry door to let the whey drip into a bowl.)*
4. Attach the ends of the cheesecloth, place it on a strainer over a bowl to collect the whey. Let drain for 2 or 3 days to firm it up. Discard the whey water.
5. The resulting cheese can be used as a spread. Add salt to taste, herbs, and mix with a fork. Form a ball and save it in a Ziplock bag.
6. Or simply cut a piece of the unflavored cheese and pour cane syrup or rhum raisin & molasses sauce on top.
7. This fresh cheese will last a week in your fridge.

n Cap-Haïtien, early morning lady street vendors will chant "Lèt Kaye" ... this is the cue to open ne door and buy from her. From all my research I could never trace this recipe in Port-au-Prince. owever, it is well known in Jeremie. The picture shows that local/ traditional delicacies can be resented/ plated like any gourmet cheese platter. *(Regular with syrup, with fresh herbs, with ashew nuts (Us in the north region we do love our cashews!).* A great substitute for ricotta.

MILK FUDG

Dous lèt is a staple in our culture. It is commonly found and appreciated. A rich sweet milky palate for sure.

Servings: 4-6

30 minutes

Dessert

MILK FUDGE (DOUS LÈT)

INGREDIENTS

1 cup of evaporated milk

1 cup of whole milk

4 cups white sugar

1 tbsp vanilla extract

2 whole cinnamon stick

1 tsp of ground nutmeg

PREP & COOK

1. In a bowl mix all the ingredients together and reserve.
2. In a pot on medium heat, cook the mixture while stirring constantly until it thickens. Remove the cinnamon stick and discard.
3. Your fudge (dous lèt) is done when a drop hardens in cold water.
4. Remove from the heat and cool the pot in a cold-water bath for 3 minutes.
5. Pour your fudge in the mold of your choice and let cool for 24 hours at room temperature.
6. As this is not a hard candy, you will be able to cut it into pieces.
7. Enjoy!

TIPS

Adding raisins soaked into rhum into the batter infuses it with another layer of flavor. You can also use plain raisins.

PEANUT FUDG

My dad and I share the same liking for this peanut fudge.

Servings: 12 +

30 minutes

Dessert

PEANUT FUDGE (DOUS PISTACH)

INGREDIENTS

1 cup peanuts

2 cup brown sugar

½ cup of milk +2 tbs of water

1 tsp ground cinnamon

1 tsp ground nutmeg

1 tbsp vanilla extract

¼ tsp salt

PREP & COOK

1. In a food processor, grind the peanuts to a fine powder consistency. Or crush in a mortar and pestle.
2. In a pot, bring to a boil the milk, water, sugar, salt, cinnamon, and spices.
3. Lower the heat and add the ground peanut to the mixture.
4. Stirs until it forms a paste.
5. Pour the paste on a wet wood cutting board large enough. Flatten to half an inch thick.
6. Let cool and cut.

TIPS

Cap -Haïtian is famous for all its fudge and several cooks left their name in the memories of many generations, I.E.: *Bazar KikiLiki* (funny name right). *Bolotte Chlotide* and her milk fudge were sold in street 7. *Libon* came later and was in street 20.

I can still close my eyes and recall the aroma of hot peanut fudge on my way back from school scrolling down street 14 H. Memories of a man behind his wooden table cutting the peanut fudge!

Replace the milk with water to get a plant-based but harder fudge.

CANDIED COCONU

ABOUT THIS RECIPE

The word Caribbean brings images of warm pristine beaches, clear blue water and makes you dream of pina colada. Did you know that this drink originates from Puerto Rico? I went to the restaurant where it was invented and had a blast!

The Caribbean equals sunny days all year-'round. We fill our afternoons with coconut ice cream, 'blanc manger', sorbets, and candied coconuts. Memories of my first bite of this candy still linger...

Servings: 12 +

30 minutes

Dessert

CANDIED COCONUT (TABLET KOKOYE)

INGREDIENTS

2 cups dried coconut thin slices

4 cups brown sugar

1 tbsp fresh grated ginger (optional)

1 pinch of salt

2 cups of water

1 tbsp vanilla extract

½ tsp baking soda

PREP & COOK

1. In a saucepan on medium heat, bring to a boil the sugar, water, ginger, and salt.
2. Once it starts boiling, remove it from the heat and add the baking soda; it will bubble immediately.
3. Add the slices of coconut immediately and mix, add the vanilla extract.
4. Pour the mixture on an oiled cookie sheet by the spoonful.
5. Let it cool and enjoy!

TIPS

f you are using fresh coconut slices, boiled them with the sugar in stage 1.

You can use a damp wood cutting board instead of the oiled cookie sheet.

CANDIED SESAME SEED

ABOUT THIS RECIPE

Sesame seeds are called jijiri in the northern part of Haïti and roroli in the other regions.

They are a good source of fiber helping to lower cholesterol levels and blood pressure.

Servings: 12 +

30 minutes

Dessert

CANDIED SESAME SEEDS (TABLET ROROLI)

INGREDIENTS

¼ cup toasted sesame seeds

½ cup of sugar

1 pinch of salt

1 tbsp of honey

1 cup of water

1 tsp of ground nutmeg

1 tsp of ground cinnamon

PREP & COOK

1. In a saucepan on medium heat, bring to a boil the sugar and water. Reduce to low heat and let it cook to a syrup consistency. About 25 minutes.
2. In a cookie sheet, place parchment paper, and oil it.
3. Once the sugar gets to the syrup stage, add the honey, cinnamon, and nutmeg.
4. Add the sesame seeds and mix well with a wooden spoon.
5. Pour the mixture on the oiled cookie sheet. Flatten it at about half an inch and let cool completely.
6. Cut the cooled mixture into diagonal-shaped portions and enjoy!

TIPS

Toasted sesame seeds can be sprinkled onto soups and salads.
When toasting the seeds, it is best to use a bit of salt to help not scorching them. Do so on medium heat and keep stirring them.
Store toasted nuts in airtight containers, they will last for weeks.

CANDIED CASHEW NUT

ABOUT THIS RECIPE

*Rapadou: sugarcane juice boiled until it becomes a thick syrup (thicker than molasses). It is unlike overly processed white **sugar** and even less processed **than** brown **sugar**, which these days is just white **sugar** colored with molasses. Rapadou is about as unprocessed as you can get. The paste is usually poured into rolls of palm leaves. They call them "kayet" in Haiti. Internationally named: Panela, rapadura or piloncillo. As a Cap-Haïtian native, not adding this treat of cashew would have been a sacrilege.

Servings: 12 +

30 minutes

Dessert

CANDIED ROASTED CASHEWS (TABLET NWA GRYE)

INGREDIENTS

2 cups of roasted unsalted cashews

½ cup rapadou*

2 cup white sugar

½ cup of water

½ tsp baking soda

½ tsp salt

1 tbsp vanilla extract

1 tbsp molasses

PREP & COOK

1. In a large saucepan, on medium heat, bring to a boil the sugar, water, vanilla extract, rapadou, molasses, and salt. When it starts to bubble, reduce to medium heat, and let it cook for about 6 minutes.
2. Remove from the heat and add the baking soda while stirring it with a wooden spoon.
3. Quickly pour the mixture on the cookie sheet.
4. Let it cool completely. Break into pieces and enjoy!

TIPS

Here is a foolish thought...If there are leftovers, store them in an airtight container. At home, they are not gone within minutes!

When you add baking soda to the sugar syrup it helps to form tiny bubbles which help with texture. You can also add butter.

No one leaves Cap-Haïtian without tasting our chicken cashew dish. No one leaves Cap-Haïtian without tasting our chicken cashew dish. It is served with black mushroom rice (diri djondjon) with cashew and lima beans.

We serve hot chocolate and Cashew with chicken puff pastry.

CANDIED PEANUT

ABOUT THIS RECIPE
Driving into Arcahaie city there is no way around the street sellers. You must get a brown paper bag of candied peanuts. You just must. "Me tablet yo, me tablet yo" "Cheri ou vle tablet?" "Fem van non" *(Here they are! Here they are! Do you want some? Take some from me!)*

Servings: 12 +

30 minutes

Dessert

CANDIED PEANUTS (TABLET PISTACH ARCAHAIE)

INGREDIENTS

2 cups of unsalted raw peanuts

2 cups of white sugar

¼ Tsp of salt

½ tsp cinnamon

1 tbsp of grated ginger

¼ Tsp lime juice or 1/4tsp of cream of tartar

½ cup of water

Ice bath

PREP & COOK

1. In a thick bottom saucepan, on medium heat, cook the sugar, water, and lime juice. Stir constantly until the sugar dissolves.
2. Bring the mix to a boil, once the mix becomes clear stop stirring immediately. Now, reduce heat to the lowest and let it simmer.
3. Let it simmer until it gets to a golden color (10-15 minutes). If you let it go to a darker color it will be bitter.
4. Remove from the heat and set the saucepan in an ice bath for 10 seconds to stop the cooking.
5. Add the peanuts mixture and mix with a wooden spoon. Pour and spread evenly on the cookie sheet with a wet rolling pin
6. Let it cool completely. Cut in pieces and enjoy!

TIPS
Unsalted store brought peanuts can be used.

PEANUT NOUGA

ABOUT THIS RECIPE

One recipe, a small difference in shape and technique, gives two different names: Nouga okap and Tablet pistach from Arcahaie

Servings: 12 +

30 minutes

Dessert

PEANUTS NOUGAT (NOUGA PISTACH)

INGREDIENTS

2 cups of unsalted raw peanuts

2 cups of white sugar

¼ Tsp of salt

½ tsp cinnamon

1 tbsp of grated ginger

¼ Tsp lime juice or 1/4tsp of cream of tartar

½ cup of water

Ice bath

Baking sheet with oiled aluminum foil to spread the hot mixture.

TIPS

Unsalted store brought peanuts can be used.

PREP & COOK

1. Preheat your oven to 325 and roast the peanuts for 15-20 minutes checking often so they do not burn.
2. Remove from the oven, let cool and peel the skin off.
3. In a bowl mix together the peanuts, ginger, cinnamon, salt, and reserve.
4. Combine the sugar, lime juice, and water into a thick bottom saucepan. Cook on medium heat while stirring constantly with a wooden spoon until the sugar dissolves.
5. Bring the mixture to a boil. At this point it should be clear, stop stirring immediately.
6. Reduce heat to medium and let the mixture simmer. It will turn from a light golden color (10-15 minutes) to amber. Do not let it get darker or it will be bitter.
7. Turn off the heat. Take the pot, and put it in the ice bath for 10 seconds to stop the cooking.
8. Add the peanuts mixture to the caramel, mix, spread immediately on your baking sheet forming a thick rectangle, use a knife and cut shapes diagonally. Let cool at room temperature until it hardens. Cut when cold in any shapes that you like.

NEW HAITIAN GASTRONOMY

The following recipe is an introduction to the "New Haïtian Gastronomy".

This recipe calls for jumbo crab meat. However, feel free to use any other crab meat that you prefer.

Servings: 04

60 minutes

Condiment

TAINO CRAB DIP (SÒS CRAB TAINO)

INGREDIENTS

- 1 lb. shredded jumbo crab meat
- 1/2 cup mayonnaise
- 1 tsp yellow mustard
- 2 tbsp diced red bell pepper
- 2 scallions chopped
- 1 tsp fresh chopped parsley
- ⅓ cup grated parmesan cheese
- ⅓ cup unsweetened coconut milk
- Pepper paste or hot sauce to taste
- Salt to taste

PREP & COOK

1. In a bowl, mix the mayonnaise, pepper paste, salt, scallions, red bell peppers, yellow mustard.
2. Then, add the coconut milk, the parmesan, and the parsley.
3. Fold in the crab meat.
4. Chill for 5 minutes.

TIPS

Serve this Dip with Accras. However, it can also go along with fresh-cut veggies.

You can use crab meat chunks from a can if you cannot find fresh crab at your local grocery store. Just make sure that you shred the meat before adding it to the sauce.

ABOUT THE AUTHOR

...er Cuisine ranges from the Taino's to the New Haïtian Gastronomy ...hich is about revisiting traditional dishes with a modern twist and promoting local, fresh, and organic products.

...hank you all for buying my cookbook. I will soon share sustain-...ble recipes and new Haïtian Gastronomy original recipes which ...re great for us and the planet. I am part of a great association called www.chefsmanifesto.com

LINKS: WWW.NATACHAGOMEZ.COM
IG: _natacha_gomez_

Made in the USA
Columbia, SC
28 April 2021